DINOSAURS

# SPINOSAURUS

BY HALEY WILLIAMS

Kids Core
An Imprint of Abdo Publishing
abdobooks.com

**abdobooks.com**



Printed in the United States of America, North Mankato, Minnesota.
102023
012024

THIS BOOK CONTAINS RECYCLED MATERIALS

Cover Photo: Daniel Eskridge/Shutterstock Images
Interior Photos: Kostiantyn Ivanyshen/Shutterstock Images, 4–5; Herschel Hoffmeyer/Shutterstock Images, 6, 28–29; Hoberman Collection/Universal Images Group/Getty Images, 7; Ingo Schulz/imageBROKER.com GmbH & Co. KG/Alamy, 8; Jose Antonio Penas/Stocktrek Images/Science Source, 10; Roger Harris/Science Source, 12–13; Michal Sanca/Shutterstock Images, 15 (human); Shutterstock Images, 15 (dinosaurs); Jose Antonio Penas/Science Source, 17; Kathy Kay/Shutterstock Images, 18; Saul Loeb/AFP/Getty Images, 20–21; Kay Nietfeld/AFP/DPA/Getty Images, 22; IFA Film/United Archives GmbH/Alamy, 25, 26

Editor: Marley Richmond
Series Designer: Mary Shaw

**Library of Congress Control Number: 2023939615**

**Publisher's Cataloging-in-Publication Data**

Names: Williams, Haley, author.
Title: Spinosaurus / by Haley Williams
Description: Minneapolis, Minnesota: Abdo Publishing, 2024 | Series: Dinosaurs | Includes online resources and index.
Identifiers: ISBN 9781098292683 (lib. bdg.) | ISBN 9798384910626 (ebook)
Subjects: LCSH: Dinosaurs--Juvenile literature. | Prehistoric animals--Juvenile literature. | Spinosaurus--Juvenile literature.
Classification: DDC 567.90--dc23

# CONTENTS

The shape of *Spinosaurus's* neck allowed the dinosaur to easily catch fish from above.

CHAPTER 1

# THE SPINED LIZARD

A *Spinosaurus* (spine-oh-SOHR-uhs) hunts in the shallow part of a river. It is searching for its next meal. Drops of water slide down the large sail along the back of the *Spinosaurus*. Its two feet squish in the mud as it walks through the flowing water.

*Spinosaurus* hunted many kinds of fish. Its diet may have included *Onchopristis*.

The swamps are full of fish for the creature to eat. It looks for the right moment. It gets ready to strike its prey.

Coelacanth are fish that lived when dinosaurs roamed Earth. They still swim in the ocean today.

Suddenly, the *Spinosaurus* dips its crocodile-like **snout** into the water. It grabs onto a coelacanth. This fish is 6.5 feet (2 m) long. It is the perfect meal for a *Spinosaurus*. The creature uses its sharp teeth and claws to rip through the skin of the fish. Once the *Spinosaurus* is finished, it continues walking through the water. It is searching for more food to eat.

Fossils show what dinosaurs may have looked like. *Spinosaurus* bones show a bit of the sail's shape.

## The Age of Dinosaurs

*Spinosaurus* is a type of dinosaur that lived millions of years ago. Dinosaurs were **prehistoric** reptiles. They came in all shapes and sizes. Dinosaurs also lived in many parts of the world. Scientists discovered dinosaurs by finding **fossils**.

Dinosaurs lived during a time known as the Mesozoic era. This period began about 252 million years ago. It ended about 66 million years ago when dinosaurs went **extinct**.

## Sauropods and Theropods

Sauropods were dinosaurs that walked on four legs. They had long necks and tails. These dinosaurs were herbivores, which means they ate only plants. Theropods were dinosaurs that walked on two legs. They were carnivores. This means they ate meat, such as other dinosaurs. *Spinosaurus* was a theropod.

Some scientists believe that *Spinosaurus* swam in rivers instead of walking through them.

The Mesozoic era was split into three parts. They are called the Triassic, Jurassic, and Cretaceous periods. *Spinosaurus* lived in the late Cretaceous period, between 95 and 70 million years ago. It is the largest meat-eating dinosaur that has ever been discovered. It could grow to be around 13 feet (4 m) longer and 8 feet (2 m) taller than *Tyrannosaurus rex.*

Some scientists believe *Spinosaurus* might have spent part of its life in water. They believe it hunted for fish. It hunted in the rivers that covered what is now North Africa.

## Explore Online

Visit the website below. Does it give any new information about the Mesozoic era that wasn't in Chapter One?

**Mesozoic**

abdocorelibrary.com/spinosaurus

Scientists aren't sure exactly what shape *Spinosaurus's* sail was. It may have dipped in the middle.

CHAPTER 2

# SPINOSAURUS CHARACTERISTICS

The name *Spinosaurus* means "spined lizard." The creature got its name from the large spines growing from its back. These spines were around 7 feet (2 m) tall. Most scientists believe the spines were connected by skin.

This made it look as though *Spinosaurus* had a sail. There are many ideas about how the sail was used. Some scientists think it could have been used for controlling body temperature or to attract a **mate**. Others think it was used for swimming.

*Spinosaurus* was about 46 to 59 feet (14–18 m) long and 14 to 20 feet (5–6 m) tall.

## Short Legs, Long Arms

*Spinosaurus* had shorter legs than most theropods. It also had longer arms. Some scientists believe *Spinosaurus* may have sometimes walked on all fours. Shorter legs and longer arms may have helped it swim better too.

# Massive Meat-Eater

A large *Spinosaurus* would have been taller and longer than a large *Tyrannosaurus rex. Spinosaurus* would have been about three and a half times taller than an average human today.

Some scientists think it weighed between 7 and 9 tons (6–8 metric tons). Others think it weighed 13 to 23 tons (12–21 metric tons).

*Spinosaurus* had a long snout similar to that of a crocodile. It also had long, cone-shaped teeth. These teeth were great for catching fish. *Spinosaurus* was known to eat smaller dinosaurs as well.

## Aquatic Dinosaur

Many scientists believe that *Spinosaurus* is one of the few dinosaurs that could swim well. However, they disagree about how much time it spent in the water. Some scientists think *Spinosaurus* was aquatic. That means it would have spent most of its life in the water.

Theropods normally have light bones. But *Spinosaurus* had dense bones. This would have helped it dive and hunt for fish better in

Discoveries have shown that *Spinosaurus* had a tail shaped like a paddle. Aquatic animals such as eels have similarly shaped tails.

deep water. Modern-day aquatic animals such as manatees have similar bones. In the 2010s and 2020s, more evidence was discovered. The first *Spinosaurus* tail fossils were found. These fossils suggest that *Spinosaurus* used its tail to move quickly through water.

To hunt for fish, herons stand very still in the water. They grab fish that swim near them. *Spinosaurus* may have hunted in a similar way.

Other scientists think that *Spinosaurus* was only semiaquatic. They say that its size and shape would have made hunting underwater difficult. *Spinosaurus's* nostrils were also far up its snout. Birds such as herons have a similar structure. That may mean *Spinosaurus* hunted in shallow water. It may have dipped its head in the water to catch a fish. But it may not have swum in deep water. However, there is still a lot that is unknown about *Spinosaurus*.

# PRIMARY SOURCE

David Martill is a scientist. He and other scientists have found many *Spinosaurus* teeth in the riverbeds of Morocco. Martill says:

> An animal living much of its life in water is much more likely to [drop teeth in] the river . . . than those dinosaurs that perhaps only visited the river for drinking and feeding.

Source: "Dino Teeth Research Prove Giant Predatory Dinosaur Lived in Water." *University of Portsmouth*, 18 September 2020. port.ac.uk. Accessed 12 Apr. 2023.

## Point of View

What is the author's point of view on this topic? What is your point of view? Write a short essay about how they are similar and different.

The National Geographic Museum in Washington, DC, had a life-sized model of a *Spinosaurus* skeleton.

CHAPTER 3

# NEW DISCOVERIES

In 1912, a German **paleontologist** named Ernst Stromer discovered an incomplete *Spinosaurus* skeleton. Stromer found the skeleton in western Egypt. The skeleton included fossils of the sail.

*Spinosaurus* fossils are very rare. Many *Spinosaurus* displays in museums use model bones to show a complete skeleton.

Stromer published his findings in 1915. He named the dinosaur *Spinosaurus*.

The fossils were later brought to a museum in Munich, Germany. During World War II

(1939-1945), Stromer asked the museum director to move the fossils. But the director refused. The museum was bombed in April 1944. The first *Spinosaurus* fossils were destroyed.

Scientists used Stromer's notes to learn more about *Spinosaurus*. But for many years, they only had small pieces of teeth and bones to study. That changed in 2008. Paleontologist Nizar Ibrahim discovered new *Spinosaurus* fossils in Morocco. Ibrahim and his team went back to the same site in 2013. They found even more fossils on that trip. Ibrahim and paleontologist Paul Sereno used the bones to create a model of a full *Spinosaurus* skeleton. In 2018 and 2019, Ibrahim's team discovered more *Spinosaurus* fossils in Morocco.

# *Spinosaurus* on Screen

*Spinosaurus* has become a well-known dinosaur in popular culture. In 2001, it was featured in the movie *Jurassic Park III.* The movie is based on a book series written by Michael Crichton. When *Jurassic Park III* was released, not much was known about *Spinosaurus.* But some of its known characteristics are shown in

### Fossils

Scientists can study fossils to see what a dinosaur might have looked like. In 2019, scientists found Spinosaurus foot bones in Morocco. The foot bones can be used to figure out whether the dinosaur had webbed feet. Knowing more about *Spinosaurus's* feet would help researchers learn more about how it spent its time in water.

*Spinosaurus* roars in *Jurassic Park III.* The moviemakers created this sound by putting together noises from a lion, an alligator, a bear, and birds.

the movie. These include its sail, longer arms, and crocodile-like snout.

*Jurassic Park III* also shows *Spinosaurus* swimming and hunting deep underwater.

In *Jurassic Park III*, a *Spinosaurus* rises out of a lake where it had been swimming underwater. It attacks a boat.

There was not a lot of evidence to support that idea when the movie was first released. New evidence of an aquatic *Spinosaurus* was later discovered. The idea has become more popular. But scientists are still not sure how much time *Spinosaurus* spent in the water.

*Jurassic Park III* introduced *Spinosaurus* to a wider audience. As fossils are found, many people want to know more. New discoveries may answer questions about the spined dinosaur.

## Further Evidence

Look at the website below. Does it give any new evidence to support Chapter Three?

**Fierce River 'Monster' *Spinosaurus***

abdocorelibrary.com/spinosaurus

# DINO DETAILS

Crocodile-like snout to help catch fish in water
Cone-shaped teeth used to rip into the skin of fish
Long arms and short legs may have been used to swim and walk on all fours

# Glossary

**extinct**
no longer exists

**fossils**
the remains of very old animals or plants

**mate**
one of two animals that breed together to create offspring

**paleontologist**
a scientist who studies fossils

**prehistoric**
having to do with the time before written history

**snout**
a long nose

# Online Resources

To learn more about *Spinosaurus*, visit our free resource websites below.

**Core Library CONNECTION**
FREE! COMMON CORE MULTIMEDIA RESOURCES

Visit **abdocorelibrary.com** or scan this QR code for free Common Core resources for teachers and students, including vetted activities, multimedia, and booklinks, for deeper subject comprehension.

**Booklinks NONFICTION NETWORK**
FREE! ONLINE NONFICTION RESOURCES

Visit **abdobooklinks.com** or scan this QR code for free additional online weblinks for further learning. These links are routinely monitored and updated to provide the most current information available.

# Learn More


Hulick, Kathryn. *Dinosaurs.* Abdo, 2023.

Johnson-Ransom, Evan. *The Dinosaur World.* Cedar Mill, 2023.

Murray, Julie. *Spinosaurus.* Abdo, 2023.

# Index



# About the Author

Haley Williams is an editor who lives in Minnesota. As a kid, she enjoyed learning about different kinds of dinosaurs.